A. Stuart

Washington Territory:

Its Soil, Climate, Productions and General Resources

A. Stuart

Washington Territory:
Its Soil, Climate, Productions and General Resources

ISBN/EAN: 9783744784559

Printed in Europe, USA, Canada, Australia, Japan

Cover: Foto ©Suzi / pixelio.de

More available books at **www.hansebooks.com**

WASHINGTON TERRITORY:

ITS

SOIL, CLIMATE, PRODUCTIONS

And General Resources.

COMPILED BY

MRS. A. H. H. STUART,

Chairman of the Board of Immigration.

———◆———

PUBLISHED BY

AUTHORITY OF THE LEGISLATURE.

———◆———

OLYMPIA:

PRINTED AT THE OFFICE OF THE WASHINGTON STANDARD.

1875.

Commissioners of Immigration

OF

WASHINGTON TERRITORY.

MRS. A. H. H. STUART,	: : ;	OLYMPIA.
HON. P. P. LACY,	: : :	WALLA-WALLA.
HON. L. B. HASTINGS,	:	PORT TOWNSEND.

PREFACE.

This work has been compiled for the purpose of aiding immigration, by describing the great natural resources of our Territory—its soil, climate, minerals, etc.

Its facts have been drawn from personal correspondence and conversation with persons living in all parts of the Territory, from published correspondence of disinterested people and from the excellent work of Messrs. Murphy & Harned, "The Puget Sound Business Directory," the Northern Pacific Railroad Company's publication, "The Settler's Guide" and the Walla Walla Immigration Society's pamphlet. The statistics of the Territory were principally furnished by the Territorial Auditor, the Hon. J. M. Murphy.

It is believed that the method of particularly describing each county by itself will give to the intending immigrant a better idea of the Territory as a whole, than a more general description as by this means he may select his locality for the business or occupation he may desire to follow.

The great need of our Territory is earnest men and women

who are not afraid or ashamed of honest work and if this little book compiled in leisure hours, may aid in bringing a healthy emigration from the older States to our Territory, its object will have been accomplished.

WASHINGTON TERRITORY.

GENERAL SKETCH.

Washington Territory, in the north-western portion of the United States, extends through nearly eight degrees of longitude, covering about three hundred and sixty miles of the frontier of British Columbia, and has an average breadth from north to south of nearly four hundred miles. It has an area of 79,128 square miles. Allowing for the waters of Puget Sound and the mountainous districts, there are 35,000,000 acres of timber, prairie and bottom land open for settlement; of these, 20,000,000 are covered with timber; 5,000,000 are rich alluvial bottom, and 10,000,000 acres are prairie and barren land.

The Territory is divided into two divisions naturally by the Cascade Mountains, which run north and south parallel with the Pacific Coast, in 45 degs. west longitude. These divisions, which are of unequal proportions, differ in soil, climate and topography. That portion lying east of the Cascades, embracing 56,213 square miles, is known as Eastern Washington. The great natural feature of this section is the Columbia River, which enters the Territory in a northern line at 41 degrees, west longitude, and pursues a westerly and southerly course for four hundred miles, until it reaches the 46th degree of north latitude, when it deflects sharply to the west, forming for about three hundred miles the boundary between the State of Oregon and Washington Terri-

tory. This noble river has great commercial advantages, fine
scenery, and can be made useful in irrigating some of the barren
plains adjacent to it, thus causing them to produce in abundance
grains and grasses. It receives in its course several rivers which
traverse this section, the principal ones of which are the Snake,
Walla Walla, Winachee, Okanagan, Spokane, Klickitat, and
others of less importance. Its principal tributary, the Snake
river, receives the waters of the Palouse, Clearwater, Tucanon
and many minor streams. These rivers have an aggregate length
within the Territory of eight hundred miles. The whole of
Eastern Washington may be denominated one vast, unbroken
prairie, for from the southern boundary of the Territory to the
Spokane river, a distance of one hundred and fifty miles, the
only prominences to be seen are the slopes of the mountains,
which are covered with evergreens. The surface is generally
high, rolling and irregular, with occasional plains. North of the
Spokane, the characteristics of the country undergo a decided
change, the balsaltic formation giving way to the slate, quartz
and limestone, and the surface breaking into hills and valleys,
covered with a good supply of various kinds of timber. This
valley, known as the Spokane, lies between the 46th and 47th
parallels; it is unfit for cultivation, the soil being a light sand,
capable of producing nothing but sage brush and a few patches
of bunch grass. The Walla Walla valley in the south-eastern
portion embraces one million acres of good arable land, capable
of supporting a large population. Land in this valley com-
mands from $5 to $40 per acre, as it is useful for either agricultural or grazing purposes. Grain is raised in large quantities,
the average yield being very high. Vegetables and fruit are
raised in profusion and of excellent quality. Beef, wheat, wool
and hides are exported from Walla Walla to Portland and San
Francisco, and its fruits and vegetables find a ready market.
There is agricultural land enough in Eastern Washington to support a large population, yet its great feature is the extensive
grazing ranges which exist in the Walla Walla, Palouse, Kliki-
tat and Yakima valleys. These ranges are covered with a profusion of bunch grass, which retains its nutritious qualities

through the winter, upon which the cattle thrive the year round. In severe winters, about one year in every eight or ten, stock must be fed and sheltered.

The principal industries of Eastern Washington is stock raising, a market being had in British Columbia, Western Washington and Oregon. Large quantities of wheat, flour and wool are annually shipped to California, the Sandwich Islands and Europe. Though the country is not heavily timbered, yet it has a good supply of cottonwood, alder, pine and cedar, which grow upon the margins of rivers and upon agricultural lands. The climate of this section is very mild for its latitude. In the Walla Walla Valley the average temperature for Spring is 52 deg.; summer, 73 deg.; in Autumn, 53 deg.; in winter, 34 deg. The average rain fall is 18 inches. Thus the climate is similar to Baltimore, Maryland. In Colville valley, further north, the winter is several degrees colder, approaching that of Northern Indiana or Ohio.

WESTERN WASHINGTON

Includes that portion lying between the Cascade Mountains on the east, the Pacific Ocean on the west, the Columbia River on the south and British Columbia on the north. It extends about four degrees of latitude and three of longitude. Its northern limit is the 49th parallel and its southern is the mid-channel of the Columbia River in latitude 45 deg., 33 min. It has an area of about 22,915 square miles, the principal part of which is heavily timbered with magnificent forests of fir, pine and cedar. Its great commercial artery is Puget Sound, which lies between the Cascade Mountains and the Pacific Ocean. It covers an area of about 2,000 square miles and has a coast line of 1,600 miles and is 120 miles in length. It is navigable for ships of the largest model, there being neither rocks or shoals from one end to the other. Vessels can find anchorage within a few hundred feet of the shore in from five to twenty fathoms of water and storms are unknown to it.

Western Washington is divided into three great basins—the Columbia, Chehalis and Puget Sound. The Columbia basin as it recedes from the river bottoms is high and broken; its soil is a mixture of clay and loam, well adapted to the production of grasses. The river bottoms are exceedingly fertile, but they are exposed to overflow during the June freshet, which often raises the Columbia from ten to twenty feet. Along the Cowlitz Valley there are large tracts of fertile land suitable for grazing or agriculture. North of the Columbia is the Chehalis basin, which embraces two thousand square miles of the best land in the Territory. This is called the garden spot of the Territory and extends from Gray's Harbor to the Cascades. The Chehalis river, which is navigable for light-draught steamers a distance of sixty miles, traverses the basin and offers the people an opportunity of getting their produce to market. This basin varies in width from fifteen to fifty miles; it is composed principally of rich bottom lands and back of this lies hills and table lands, useful for grazing and cultivation. A large body of rich land also, lies along the Willopah river, an important stream emptying into Shoalwater Bay. The Puget Sound basin proper, embracing about 1,200 square miles, has a varied soil, portions being gravelly, but along its numerous water courses rich alluvial deposits exist. The basin is supposed to be one vast field of coal, as croppings have been found in almost every locality where it has been sought for. It is bountifully supplied with excellent rivers and streams, which empty into the Sound, offering unusual facilities for internal navigation, as many of them are navigable for small steamers for several miles from their mouths.

The productions of Western Washington are hay and the grains and fruit common to a temperate climate except corn and peaches, which are raised only in favored localities. No country is better for cereals and fruits, especially berries, which grow in great profusion, many of the varieties being unknown in the Eastern States. Hops are cultivated in some localities and yield abundantly, and from their peculiar excellence and size find a ready market in San Francisco for foreign exportation. Though the summers are comparatively dry, drouths are unknown, as are also destructive insects.

The climate of Western Washington is of very even temperature. There are really but two seasons, the wet and the dry; the former beginning in November and lasting until April, and the latter occupying the remainder of the year. The average temperature for the wet season is 39 degrees; for the dry, 63 degrees. Occasionally for a few days in summer the thermometer marks 90 degrees, but the nights are always cool.

Lumber and coal are the principal articles of export. There are sixteen lumber mills on the Sound engaged in its production, having a capacity of from 30,000 to 100,000 feet each, per day, while at Seattle, Bellingham Bay and other points, numerous coal mines are open and many thousand tons are being shipped to San Francisco yearly. It is estimated that 300,000,000 feet of lumber are manufactured annually in our Territory, valued at $3,000,000. Ship building is carried on extensively, and no country in the world offers greater facilities for this business than the Puget Sound basin. The exportation of fish is also destined at no distant day to become a prominent business, for fish of many varieties and excellent quality abound in the waters of the Territory, and the rich yielding fishing grounds of the north are more convenient to the Territory than any other part of the United States; the climate is better fitted for curing and drying than any other part of the Pacific Coast, and finally, shipping can be built cheaper on the Sound than elsewhere on the Continent.

The population of the Territory is estimated at 36,000, of, which 12,000 are in Eastern Washington and the remainder in Western Washington. Except in Colville Valley, there are but few inhabitants in the north-eastern part of the Territory, but settlements exist in nearly all parts of Western Washington. The school and school laws are excellent and the Territory offers educational facilities which are very superior, considering its limited population. A Territorial University is located at Seattle, and the towns have excellent public and private schools. The roads of the Territory extend to all portions of it where settlements have been made.   The Northern Pacific Railroad, it is hoped, will be completed from one end of the Territory to the other in a few years, and this, when done, will open communication with the different sections and afford a much needed means of transportation for the products of the interior to a good market.

HEALTHFULNESS OF CLIMATE.

The equable temperature, combined with the invigorating breezes from the Pacific Ocean, makes the Territory one of the most healthy localities in the Union.   In comparing the mortality lists, it will be seen that Washington shows the least number of deaths.   The rate of mortality in Arkansas is one person out of every forty-eight; Massachusetts and Louisiana, one out of every fifty-seven; Illinois and Indiana, one in eighty-seven; Kansas, one in sixty-eight; Vermont, the healthiest State on the Atlantic slope, one in ninety-two; California, one in one hundred and one; Oregon, one in one hundred and seventy-two, and Washington Territory, one in two hundred and twenty-eight.

PRODUCTIONS.

The productions of Washington Territory are as varied as the soil and climate.   Among the first may be classed timber, coal, cereals and fruit.   The Walla Walla and Colville valleys are peculiarly adapted to the growth of wheat.   Seventy or eighty bushels have been raised to the acre, but the average yield is about thirty-five.   Corn is also raised here and peaches, which in Western Washington grow only in scattered localities, attain in Eastern Washington a large size and good flavor.   The extensive grazing ranges of Walla Walla, Palouse and Yakima Valleys are covered with bunch grass, and on this, thousands of cattle, sheep and other domestic animals feed.   Western Washington produces all that the eastern section does except corn and peaches, the climate not being warm enough to ripen these The fruit trees bear earlier here than in the East, and their products are superior, being large and juicy. Small fruits of all varities grow in profusion, and large quantities are annually shipped to the States further South. The cranberry is the most profuse of the berries natural to the country, patches occupying an area, in some localities, of from one to five square miles. Grapes do not grow here in any quantity, on account of the cool nights. The humidity of the climate is favorable to the production of grasses, which attain a height unknown on the Atlantic seaboard. As the cold, even in the most severe winter, is of short duration, these grasses flourish the year round, affording sweet and nutritious feed for cattle at all seasons, and this fact renders the dairy business a very profitable one. The butter of this Territory has an almost national reputation for its density and flavor. Vegetables, too, attain a size and abundance scarcely creditable. It is by no means an uncommon occurrence to gather from 500 to 1,000 bushels of potatoes per acre. Onions will average 800 bushels on selected ground; turnips from 700 to 1,000 bushels; parsnips and carrots about the same, and cabbage yields upon such land, twenty thousand pounds to the acre.

THE AVERAGE RAIN FALL

In the Puget Sound basin is forty inches; at Cape Disappointment, near the mouth of the Columbia river, 108 inches, and at Cape Flattery, at the mouth of the Straits of San Juan de Fuca, 130 inches.

COMMERCE AND MANUFACTURES.

The commerce of the Territory is rather limited, owing to the sparseness of its population, the want of rapid means of communication, and the non-developement of its resources. The exports are lumber, coal, wheat, flour, barley, oats, fruits, horned cattle, horses, sheep, hides, wool, furs and fish. Of these the principal one is lumber and in this an extensive trade is carried on with California, South America, the Sandwich Islands, China and Australia. There are sixty mills in the Territory engaged in its manufacture, and of these, sixteen are located on Puget Sound. The latter export the principal portion of their product, the remainder only manufacturing to supply the local demand. The Territory is now the chief lumber mart of the Pacific coast, and as the rivers are opened up and population increases the trade must become enormous. Along the banks of many of the rivers emptying into the Sound there are large tracts of excellent timber, which can be rafted at small expense to tide-water. The next leading article of export in Western Washington is coal, which is shipped from the mines at Bellingham Bay, Lake Washington, and many others, which are being opened with great rapidity and promise an enormous yield. This coal is principally of a bituminous nature, though prospectors in Puyallup valley and Green River, claim to have found fine deposits of anthracite coal. The mine at Lake Washington yields about two hundred tons per day, and sells at eleven dollars per ton in San Francisco, where it is principally shipped. The exports of this mine alone amounts to between three and four hundred thousand dollars yearly. The mine at Bellingham Bay is the most extensive in the Territory and is capable of supplying any quantity required for the trade of the Coast. It now yields one hundred and twenty-five thousand tons annually. A splendid quarry of blue sandstone is also worked at Bellingham Bay, but not to its full capacity. Another quarry of gray sandstone lies near Port Townsend, and several others of fine quality may be found in different parts of the Territory. The principal exports of Eastern Washington are flour, wheat, and the various grains, cattle, hides, wool and fruit, but no statistics can be gathered of their value which must be very large. The exportation of canned and smoked salmon from the fisheries along the Columbia river and at other points, is very heavy and promises soon to become one of the greatest industries in the Territory. The product of the eight canning establishments on the Washington Territory side of the Columbia River for 1875 was 147,500 cases containing two dozen two-pound cans each, and several minor fishing posts shipped about 20,000 barrels. This business employs a large number of hands and pays a handsome profit to those engaged in it, as the expenses are very insignificant when compared with the gross returns. An extensive trade in oysters is carried on between Shoalwater Bay and San Francisco and Portland. The shipment is estimated to be as much as 100,000 baskets a year, and as the wholesale price of this bivalve is one dollar per basket, the value of the exports of this business alone are $100,000. Large quantities of a specie of sardine, which ascends the Cowlitz river late in the Autumn, are also caught and shipped to Portland, beside sturgeon, which are shipped largely in the Fall. The total exports of the Territory will probably reach six millions of dollars per annum, while the imports do not reach more than half that sum.

The manufactures of this Territory are extremely limited, and it may be said to have scarcely any, notwithstanding its splendid water power, its profusion of timber and extensive coal fields. With the exception of lumber, there is no other leading product manufactured. A few tanneries and door and sash factories, a few furniture factories and a foundry or two exist, but these are not sufficient to supply the local demand. The former business, which would pay well, as hides are cheap, might be started in a dozen places, and everything manufactured would find a ready market in San Francisco. There is but one woolen mill in the Territory, situated at Dayton, in Columbia County, which manufactures 200,000 pounds of wool per year, to the value of between $50,000 and $60,000 yearly. With ample water power on any of the principal streams, wool in large quantities, such enterprises all over the country would pay large returns on the necessary investment. The only iron works in the Territory, are small shops at Seattle and Port Madison, on Puget Sound, notwithstanding the fact that the large number of mills and steamers owned here have repairing enough to keep many of large size employed. As a consequence, much of the repairing is done in San Francisco, Portland and Victoria which should be done within our own borders.

SHIPPING.

The shipping interests of the Territory are constantly increasing. Ere many years shall have elapsed, Puget Sound will be the ship building mart of the Pacific Coast, as it possesses unequaled facilities for such business. Its forests of fir, pine and cedar extend from the Cascade Mountains to the Pacific Ocean, an area of about 40,000 square miles. Many of these trees have an altitude of three hundred feet and a diameter of twelve feet, and yield 800,000 feet of lumber. The yellow fir, which grows on the Pacific Coast from the 42d to the 54th parrallel, is used principally for the construction of vessels, as it is the most durable and strongest timber on the Coast. Experiments made with this wood in the dock yards of Toulon, France, prove it to be far superior to any other for masts and spars. The report made of it states, that " the principal quality of this wood is a flexibility and tenacity of fibre and exceptional dimensions, strength, lightness and absence from knots." This report is true in every particular. The fir used will often furnish spars one hundred and fifty feet long, devoid of sap or knots, and planks ranging from sixty to ninety feet in length, can be procured with facility. It also makes most excellent ship frames, knees, spars and holds fastening longer and better than the acidulous oak. Many of the finest river steamers and sea-going vessels on the Coast have been built of this wood, and they have proven as staunch as those made of the famed oak. The yellow cedar is another valuable timber for ships. The Indians make their canoes of it, as it fine grained, flexible and dense. It makes excellent ship decks. Its usual height is about one hundred and fifty feet; its diameter from three to four feet. In 1871, the Territory owned 91 sailing vessels of 20,509.15 tonnage; 24 steam vessels of 2,019.59 tonnage. In 1872, sixteen vessels were built aggregating 679 tons. In 1873, ten vessels were built with a capacity of 1,052 tons. In 1874, twenty vessels were built with a carrying capacity of 4,350 tons.

MINERALOGY.

No complete geological or mineralogical reports having been made of the Territory by a competent scientist, the abundance and variety of the minerals are comparatively unknown. Quartz bearing a small quantity of gold, has been found in several localities and a few placer mines have been worked to a small extent, on the tributaries of the Columbia River and near Fort Colville. Traces of silver, lead, iron and copper have also been found, but their extent has not yet been tested. In coal, however, the Territory is very wealthy; the whole of the Puget Sound basin is supposed to be one vast coal field, and wherever it has been prospected, rich developments have been found. All the coal discovered has proven to have good heating power, and an engineer of many years experience has stated that he preferred the coal of this Territory to any other found on the Coast for puposes of steam. Washington has been appropriately termed the "Pennsylvania of the Pacific."

FORESTS.

Washington Territory is unquestionably the timber land of the Pacific Coast, about two-thirds of its area being covered with the most magnificent forests on the Continent. The shrubbery and flora of the Territory are also abundant, and many species o the latter unknown to the Atlantic Coast are found here. First among the varities of wood are the coniferous trees, which are most abundant. Of these the red and black fir, stand prominent not only in profuseness but utility. The foliage of the fir resembles the Canadian white spruce, but the leaves are larger. It is rather coarse grained and liable to shrink, but its adaptability to bear rough weather makes it good lumber. It is also very resinous, and this makes it excellent fire wood. The yellow fir if limited to the country between the Cascades and the Coast Ranges. Its foliage is darker and denser, its branches shorter and it is finer grained and more elastic than the other firs. The black spruce grows on marshes and tide-water lands and in appearance it resembles the Norway spruce. It does not grow so tall as the fir but it is often eight feet in diameter. The wood is very strong and tough, which makes it useful for spars and masts. The Oregon cedar is found throughout the country. Its diameter ranges from ten to fifteen feet. Being light, soft and durable it is used extensively for rails and shingles. It is exported largely. The hemlock spruce is also found here in various localities, but nowhere does it form a forest of itself. It grows to a height of one hundred and fifty feet with a diameter of from six to eight feet. The Oregon yew resembles the European yew and generally grows in damp soil. Its wood is tough and elastic and is used by the Indians for the manufacture of bows. It is about fifty feet high and from one to two feet in diameter. A species of pine grows on the edge of sandy prairies and along the sea beach and attains a height of fifty feet and a diameter of two feet. The spruce is also found along the Sound. The yellow pine grows to majestic proportions in Eastern Washingon. The white pine is found along the Sound, where it is used for lumber. A species of arbor-vitæ grows along the Straits of Fuca. The oak grows in several localities, but where it approaches the evergreen it is crowded out and stunted by the towering firs. It seldom grows over fifty feet high and three in diameter and is inferior to the principal species in the Atlantic States. The maple grows luxuriantly. It is different from any Eastern species and is the most beautiful of its family in North America. It is frequently eighty feet high and attains a diameter of six feet with smooth bark and pale, green leaves from six to twelve inches in breadth. Its wood is superior in beauty of veining and is capable of high polish. Sugar has been made from its sap, and may yet become an important product. The vine-maple grows twenty-five to thirty feet high and a foot through, and is used largely for fuel. Two species of alder are found here, one of which attains a height of sixty feet. The wood being white and soft is good for carving or furniture. The Oregon ash inhabits moist, sandy soil or river banks. It is larger than the ash on the Atlantic Coast and is light and elastic. The dogwood grows principally between the Cascade and Coast Ranges, and the wood is tough and strong. The beautiful laurel tree is found on the Straits of Fuca and on the gravelly banks of the Sound, but is not found west of the Coast Range. It attains a height of forty feet and a diameter of two feet, and is very valuable owing to its strength, heaviness and capacity to receive a brilliant polish. There are three species of poplar, the most abundant of which is the aspen. Several varieties of willow grow along the river banks, but only two attain the size of trees, they being generally about thirty feet high. The wild cherry grows in several localities to the height of thirty feet, but is but little valued. The crab-apple, in many localities, form orchards on the prairies. Its presence is an indication of good soil. The wood is hard and tough and the fruit well flavored. A birch is common about the Straits of Fuca, and a species of the buckthorn, which grows thirty feet in height and is found in ravines and on mountain sides. It has no special value as a wood. The mild climate and humid atmosphere causes the trees in this Territory to grow with more rapidity than on the Eastern coast, and to bear their fruits earlier. The foliaceous trees assume their Spring garb and are as gaily decked in March as their kindred of the East in May.

FLORA.

Four hundred species of plants, which are indigenous to the Territory, have been collected, but these do not embrace onefourth of the number, for no collection has been made of the alpine and sub-alpine flora. All the plants growing in the valleys have been found as high as the snow line on the mountains, diminished, of course, in size. The floras of Eastern and Western Washington are dissimilar, owing to the differences in soil and climate. Of the four hundred varieties collected in this Territory, about one hundred and fifty are indigenous to the prairies. The Western portion of the Territory has the largest share of the flora, but many of the Eastern are exceedingly fragrant and brilliant. The principal Spring flowering plants commence sprouting early, and are as far advanced in February as their kindred

B

on the Atlantic coast in May. The sandy prairies along the sea beach contain many varieties of plants not found elsewhere in the country. If Persia deserves the name of the land of roses, Washington Territory is entitled to the name of the home of flowers, for they spring up in every spot where they can find growing room, from the loftiest Cascades to the gloomiest recesses of the forests.

FISH.

The fishing grounds of the Northwest coast are the most prolific on the Continent, and the variety of fish they contain is on par with their extent. Whale are found from Washington Territory to the Arctic Ocean. She principal salt water fish used for the table, such as cod, halibut and sturgeon, are numerous along the coast to the extreme northern limit of Alaska, while salmon and trout of fine quality are in all the rivers and streams. Of the principal species of fish peculiar to the Territory, the salmon holds the first place in numbers and commercial value, the Sound and the Columbia and their continuous waters and tributaries fairly swarming with them in the spawning season. There are twelve varieties of this fish known from the spring silver salmon, averaging twenty-five pounds in weight, to the salmon trout, which weighs about five pounds. Beside the salmon family, there are other exceedingly edible varieties of both fresh and salt water fish, among which is the Puget Sound cod. This weighs four or five pounds and is of excellent quality. The rock cod, a fine table fish, bites freely at a bated hook and makes good fishing. A fish known as the tom cod, about the size of a trout, is found at certain seasons. Two varieties of the perch are found here, the golden-barred perch and the viviparous. The carp is also abundant but comparatively worthless. Herring of excellent quality enter Shoalwater Bay, in immense schools, in June and are found throughout the summer in the Sound and the Straits of Fuca. Another specie of fish very abundant is the celebrated anchovy, which are taken in large numbers on the flats of Shoalwater Bay during the Summer. The sturgeon, turbot, skate, chub, killy, plaice and stickleback can be found in the Sound. Halibut of large size are found in the Straits and along the northern coast. With the fish we may mention the mollusca and cretacea, which are very abundant. Of the former there are eighty species, the most important of which are the oyster, clam, razor-fish, mussel, quohog and periwinkle. The former shell-fish is cultivated extensively at Shoalwater Bay and shipped largely. It may also be found at the mouth of Hood's Canal and Nisqually river, and one or two other localities. The clam is found in all the salt waters of the Territory and is used extensively as an article of food. There are twelve varieties of the crutacea in Puget Sound and Shoalwater Bay, the most important of which is the crab, lobster and craw-fish. The shrimp is found in a few places, but it does not attain the size of its kindred further south. It will be seen that the advantages of the Territory over any part of the Pacific Coast, for the prosecution of the fishery business are many and very apparent.

ANIMALS.

The zoology of the Territory is as extensive and varied as its other products. Not only are the animals numerous, but many of them are strangers to the country east of the Rocky Mountains. The Territory is a paradise to the hunter, for in every portion of it, it is a matter of choice which he shall pursue. In enumerating the animals we shall give the black bear the first position. It is known to the Indian by the name of itsoot, and is found throughout the wooded portions of the Territory, where it subsists upon berries and roots. His flesh is excellent, and he is the only variety of this family that is found in the Territory, except an occasional straggler of the grizzly specie, found east of the Cascades. The cougar is found extensively. Large numbers are killed annually on account of its depredations on stock. It is the only member of the feline race which takes voluntarily to water, when desiring to cross a stream. Two other animals of this specie, which are abundant and destructive to the farm-yard, are the red-cat and the American wild-cat. They live principally on birds, field mice, etc. Of the wolf there are three species, the gray, dusky and prairie wolf or cayote. These are very numerous from the Cascades to the Rocky Mountains, but west of the former range the dusky wolf is most abundant. The cayote is found principally in Eastern Washington. Five species of the deer family are common. Of these the elk is the largest. It inhabits the heavy timbered sections from the Cascades to California, and is plenty in Coast Range. Numbers of them are found near the large rivers, in the winter season, when driven from the mountains by snow. The Virginia deer is found along the borders of the prairies, but the black-tailed deer is the most numerous, found west of the Cascades. The red deer is frequent on the coast. The mule deer is found east of the Cascades and a specie of Albino deer is found on Whidby Island. The mountain goat and big-horn sheep are inhabitants of the Cascade Mountains, and it is said that in jumping from a high place he alights on his horns, none the worse for the leap. The beaver and the otter are very plentiful, the first on the minor streams flowing from the Cascade Mountains, and the second on the coast. There are six varieties of the fox. The red hare is abundant, also, the black-footed racoon. The mole, weasel, mink, pine marten, pole-cat, badger, several species of squirrel and the yellow-footed marmot, abound. An animal known as the swellel by the Indians, about thirteen inches long, of a reddish brown color and a short tail, has an extensive range from the Cascades to the sea coast. It lives in colonies, in burrows, and subsists on berries and roots. Indians use its flesh for food. The pouched rat is abundant on the gravelly plains. The wood rat is common and the musk rat is found round the lakes and streams.

BIRDS.

Like the quadrupeds, the birds of the Territory are numerous. There are nine kinds of hawk common to the country. The bald or white-headed eagle is the most numerous of the falcon tribe, and is a constant resident. The osprey is also abundant in the summer season. Of the owl family we have the horned owl, the mottled owl, the short-eared owl, the long-eared owl, the gray owl, the saw-whit and the pigmy owl. Several of these are constant residents. There are seven species of woodpecker of various sizes and plumage. They are very numerous. The most common of the humming birds, is the red-backed, which arrives in April and tarries until September. The goat-suckers, swifts, nighthawks, kingfishers, kingbirds and pewees, blue jays and magpies, are abundant. The various species of thrushes, wrens, robins, wagtails, warblers, swallows, martins, larks, finches, sparrows, linnets, orioles, blackbirds and sprikes are numerous. The raven and fish-crow are a constant inhabitant of Puget Sound, and the nut-cracker, another of this family, frequents the Cascades. The band-tailed and common dove frequent the central portion of the Territory. Those excellent sporting birds, the grouse and pheasant are very abundant, of which there are five species of the former. The grouse inhabit the highlands and the pheasant the marshes and swamps. Quail have been introduced into the Territory, but their destruction is at present prevented by law. The sage hen is found in Eastern Washington, and the plumed partridge, but the latter only in small coveys. The acquatic and wading birds are very numerons. There are four varieties of the crane and four species of the plover. A bird peculiar to the northern portion of Puget Sound is the oyster-catcher. There are two kinds of turnstone, ten of snipe and two of the phalarope. Of the swan there are two species, which are found extensively on the Columbia River and the various lakes during the winter. There are three specimens of the wild goose, which are excellent eating. Brants are common, ducks in almost numberless quantities, pelicans, cormarants, albatross, gulls, loons, kittiwakes, grebes, auks and puffins are numerous. Many of them have fine plumage.

REPTILES.

The Territory is comparatively free from reptiles, and a curious fact is, that in Western Washington there is not a poisonous reptile of any kind. Rattlesnakes are met with at the top of the Cascade Mountains, thence easterly, but none approach to the west. There are a few lizards, salamanders and toads. The garter snake and a small headed striped snake, both harmless, are sometimes seen. The entire extent of the ophidions in this country is not more than six or seven species, most of which are harmless.

MOUNTAINS,

The most marked topographical feature of Washington Territory is its magnificent, snow-clad mountain ranges. The principal of these is the the Cascade Range, an extension of the Sierra Nevada Mountains, which follow the coast northward from Lower California until they are lost in British Columbia. This range rivals the Rocky Mountains in the altitude of many of its peaks. It is the dividing line between Eastern and Western Washington. The other is the Coast Range, not so high as the former, but its rugged and many-peaked outlines, covered with perennial snow, are visible from all portions of the Sound and add a charm to its scenery. These mountains are covered with great forests, of fir to the snow line. Ranging from the north are the following snowy peaks of the Cascade Mountains: Baker, with an altitude of 11,100 feet; Rainier, 14,444; St. Helens, 9,750; Hood, 14,000; Jefferson, 10,200; McLaughlin or Pitt, 11,000. The highest of these, Rainier, is conspicuous both in Washington and Oregon. The Coast Range follows the coast; it is generally a region of hills, peaks and ridges, rising from a a few hundred, to six or seven thousand feet. Its highest peak, bearing the classical name of Mount Olympus, has an altitude of 8,100 feet and is the most conspicuous of the range. These two ranges have a varied character, and some of the peaks give occasional indications of ther volcanic origin, by spirting columns of smoke.   Another range, the Blue Mountains, form the western boundary of the Snake river region.   From the Columbia to Fort Colville, it is interrupted by level tracts, but north of this place is a range of heights which extend west to the Columbia river and may be considered a part of the general chain.   The Peaks Mountains may be numbered with the preceeding, as they lie west of the Rocky Mountains.   The elevation of the Blue Mountains is from eight to nine thousand feet, but near Walla Walla it decreases to five thousand feet.   These mountains are the source of many rivers and streams which water the Territory so generally and thoroughly.

HARBORS.

The Territory is admirably supplied with harbors, the safest and best in the world.   The whole of Puget Sound may be called one vast harbor, land-locked and secured from storms by the mountain ranges which environ it, and deep enough for the largest ship to float.   All the harbors on the Sound are of a semicircular form, and vary from two to eight miles in length and from one to six miles in breadth, and all have broad entrances, bold shores and when a ship enters one, she is as safe as if she were in a pond.   On the coast, the first harbor north of the mouth of the Columbia river is Shoalwater Bay, so named on account of the shallowness of the water at low tide.   It is the receptacle of several streams, the largest of which is the Willopah.   It is fifteen miles long, has an average width of three miles and a half, and is situated in latitude 46 deg., 36 min. and 45 sec., north, and 124 deg. west from Greenwich.   The next harbor is Gray's Harbor.   Its entrance is between Point Hanson and Eld Island, and here a heavy serf is always breaking, so that without a pilot, it is not always safe for vessels to enter.   The Copalis, Chehalis, Tyso, Chinois and Humptolups rivers empty into it.   Of these, the largest is the Chehalis, which is navigable for sixty miles by light-draught steamers.   Neah Bay, on the

Straits of Fuca, is the first harbor inside of Cape Flattery. It is a mile and a quarter long and has the same breath of entrance, but it is somewhat protected by a small island on the straits side. During a westerly wind it is exposed, and a heavy swell rolls in, but no other winds effect it. A village of the Makaw Indians is located here. Clallam Bay, situated twenty-five miles east of Cape Flattery, is semicircular in form and two miles wide. Good anchorage can be found here. Port Angeles, east of the preceeding, is an excellent harbor, when once inside it, but it is difficult to leave without the favor of wind and tide. Eight miles from the last is New Dunginess Bay, a good harbor, having deep and safe anchorage, and safe from all the storms except a south-east wind in the Straits, which blows directly into it. Squim Bay, six miles and a half from the preceeding is three miles long and one mile wide. Port Discovery, nine miles from Squim Bay, has but one fault and that is its great depth of water, which ranges from twenty-five to forty fathoms. Its average width is a mile and three-quarters and its length nine miles. Its shores are bold and heavily timbered. The next harbor inside this is Port Townsend, but it may be classified with Puget Sound. Of Puget Sound, not much more need be said, it having been described in general terms before. The Straits of Juan de Fuca require a brief notice. The entrance to the Straits from the Pacific Ocean, lies between Cape Flattery in Washington Territory and Cape Bonilla on Vancouver Island, and is twelve miles wide. The Straits run in a direct line east for forty miles, having a uniform width of eleven miles, then contracts to eight miles between Beechy Head and Striped Peak, thence runs a little north of east for fifteen miles, thence changes to a northward course, expanding to a width of twenty miles and dividing into two sub-channels, the Straits of Rosario and Canal de Haro, which leads through the Archipelago de Haro, northward to the Gulf of Georgia. From the Ocean to Whidby Island, which terminates it on the east, the mid-channel distance is eighty-four miles. It passes into Puget Sound in the southeast, and is the principal artery for the preceeding and their adjuncts, Possession Sound, Bellingham Bay, Hood's Canal and the Gulf of Georgia, which extends northward 120 miles.   The depth of the water is very great, no soundings having been found in its deepest part, with 150 fathoms of line.   Bellingham Bay, south of Rosario Straits, has an entrance two miles in width, which contracts to one mile off Cyprus Island.   There are several islands in the channel called the Cone Islands.   It is fourteen miles long and three wide, a depth of water from three to twenty fathoms and a general direction from south-east to north-west. Hood's Canal empties into Puget Sound near Port Gamble. The following is the shore line of the principal bodies of water, in nautical miles:

Straits of Juan de Fuca..161
Gulf of Georgia, Canal de Haro and Rosario Straits................627
Puget Sound..614
Hood's Canal..192

Total..1,594

RIVERS.

The Territory is profusely watered by rivers, varying in size from the noble Columbia to the tiny mountain brooklet.   Western Washington is more liberally watered than the Eastern division.   These rivers with few exceptions, have their sources in the Cascades and Coast ranges, and owing to the vast quantities of snow which melts and swells them, they are very cold and clear. In most of them table trout can be found and they are the resort of a large number of wild geese, ducks and swan.   The most fertile land in the Territory is to be found along these river bottoms and it is the abundance of these rivers that render the principal portion of the Territory so desirable for farming lands.   The first of these rivers in extent and commercial importance is the Columbia, which rises in the Rocky Mountains, in latitude 50 deg. 20 min.   After flowing northerly for nearly two degrees, it deflects sharply to the south and in latitude 51 deg., expands into a series of small lakes.   A few miles further south it receives the waters of the Kootnai, Spokane and several minor streams. Where it receives the waters of the Okanagan, it turns almost

due west for several miles, then turning south it receives the
waters of the Wenachee, Chelan, Methon, Enteathwa, Yakima,
Klickitat, Walla Walla and Snake rivers, the latter being its
main tributary. The Snake river receives the Palouse, Clearwater and Tucanon rivers, and several of less importance, all of
which go to swell the Columbia. This splendid river, whose
tributaries alone have a length of eight hundred miles in the Territory, is 1,300 miles long. It is navigable for heavy ships 115
miles, and for river steamers 160 miles from its mouth. A portage of a few miles interrupts navigation, when it is again resumed,
and thence up Snake river, until the summer season, when the
waters become too low. The Columbia is the dividing line between Washington and Oregon for a distance of 300 miles. The
most northern of the rivers which flow through Western Washington is the Nooksahk, which has its source northeast of Mount
Baker. It empties into Bellingham Bay and its total length is
forty-six miles. Some excellent land can be found near it, and
coarse gold has been found on one of its tributaries. South of
this, and emptying into the same bay is the Samish river,
another pretty stream. The Skagit river rises in the Cascades
near the 49th parallel, and empties into Port Susan. It is the
most important river of the Puget Sound basin. It drains a region extending one degree of latitude, but its navigation is prevented by a jam of fallen trees whose branches are so closely in-
terlaced as to prevent the passage of a canoe. The obstruction
once cleared away, the river is navigable for light-draught steamers a distance of sixty miles, and will open to settlers some of the
most fertile land of the Territory. The Stillaguamish river also
empties into Port Susan. It is forty miles long and flows in a
westerly course. This is somewhat obstructed by drift wood,
which, if it were removed, would render the river navigable for
twenty miles for small steamers. Excellent land skirts its banks
and croppings of coal have been found in localities adjacent to it.
The next rivers towards the south are the Snohomish and Snoqualmie. Extensive cranberry marshes are found at the mouth
of the former. The banks of this river are subject to inundation
during the annual freshet, but back of them lie excellent land

which can be easily cleared. · The Snoqualmie rises in the Cascades, at an altitude of three thousand feet, and flows in an easterly direction for twenty miles, where it makes a plunge of two hundred and seventy feet, forming the celebrated Snoqualmie Falls, then joins the Snohomish and becomes blended with it until it reaches the sea, a distance of forty miles. Another branch of the Snohomish is called the Skywamish. The Duwamish river, which receives the waters of several tributaries, empties into Elliot Bay, near Seattle. The principal of these branches are the White and Green rivers. The total length of the Duwamish, including White River, which is the fountain head, may be estimated at sixty-two miles. In this vicinity are several other rivers of importance, Black River, the outlet of Lake Washington and Cedar River, near which are some excellent agricultural lands open to settlement. The Duwamish is navigable for thirty miles. The Puyallup rises near Mount Rainier, flows in a north-westerly direction for forty miles and empties into Commencement Bay. · The valleys adjoining the river are extremely fertile and yield heavy crops of hops, grain, etc. It is the principal hop region of the Territory at present, and this year, (1875) yielded about 200,000 pounds. Extensive coal deposits have also been found here, and the only vein of what is claimed to be anthracite, are among these. The Nisqually river rises south of Mount Ranier, flows in a northwesterly direction for eighty miles, receiving in its course several streams, and empties into Puget Sound, eleven miles from Olympia. Several streams water the western side, the principal of which is the Skokomish, which rises in the Coast Range and empties into Hood's canal, about twenty-eight miles from Olympia. The valley adjoining is extremely fertile and produces abundant crops. The Quillehute rises in the Coast Range and empties into the Pacific Ocean. It is navigable for canoes for several miles, and the valley adjoining, which bear its name, offers great inducements to the farmer and stock-raiser and its richness of soil is equal to any land in the Territory. The Quinault River empties into the ocean a few miles north of Port Granville. The largest river south of this is the Chehalis, which rises in the Cascade Mountains and empties into Gray's Harbor, eighty miles from its source.   It receives the waters of the Newaukum, Skookum Chuck, Satsop, Westican, Black, Johns and Wynooche.   The region of country which it waters is called the " Garden Spot" of the Territory, and it merits the name.   Prairies, good for grazing, are abundant, and agricultural land, which only needs the hand of the husbandman to yield plentifully, await the industrious settler.   The Copalis river also empties into Gray's Harbor.   It mouth is nearly closed by a bar.   The Willopah, Palux and Nasal rivers empty into Shoalwater Bay, the principal one of which is the Willopah, which enters the north-east part.   It is nine miles wide at its mouth and the oldest settlement in the Territory is located on its banks.   The Palux enters five miles north-east of Leadbetter Point and its greatest width is a half a mile.   The Nasal enters eleven miles from the preceeding, and is rather deep, having twenty feet of water at its mouth.   The most important stream entering on the north side of the bay is the Necomanche, which is a mile and a half wide at high' tide.   Of the streams emptying into the lower Columbia river, the most important are the Cowlitz, Lewis, Washougal and Cathlapootle.   The first rises in the Cascade Mountains between Mount Rainier and St. Helens, flows in a varying course from south-west to south and empties into the Columbia opposite the town of Rainier.   It is one hundred miles long, is navigable for steamers for twenty-four miles and for canoes much further.   A fine farming country is watered by it. Lewis river rises in the southern part of the Territory and enters the Columbia opposite St. Helens.   The Washougal seeks its outlet twelve miles from Vancouver and the Cathlapootle eighteen miles below it.

LAKES.

There are innumerable lakes scattered throughout the Territory, the largest and most important of which is Lake Washington, in King County and lying three miles back of Seattle. It has a length of twenty miles and an average width of three

miles and a half. It is separated from Lake Union, which lies
between it and the Sound, by a portage of one-fourth of a mile,
which could be easily cut away and both lakes run into one.
From Lake Union to the Sound it is but one mile, and as
the ground is sloping towards the latter, a canal could be cut for
a small sum and thus the vast bodies of timber and fine agricultural land be made accessible by direct water communication
from the Sound. In Pierce County, four miles from Steilacoom,
is situated American Lake, a fine body of water and next to this
Gravelly and Steilacoom lakes, which form a chain, being but
little apart. Whatcom Lake in Whatcom County, is another
beautiful sheet of water about nine miles long. Nearly all the
lakes of the country abound in fine fish which bite readily.

LANDS.

Lands fit for cultivation or grazing can be found in most parts
of the Territory, either under the homestead and pre-emption
acts or by purchase. Not more than one per cent. of the land is
under cultivation, but the cause of this is easily traced to the
sparseness of the population. Of the entire area, not more than
ten million acres are prairie and barren land, but the prairies
though composed of a sandy, gravelly soil, are good for grazing,
and many produce good crops and a large extent of the barren
land could be reclaimed by irrigation. There are thirty-five million acres of timber land, all of which, or nearly all, is good farming land, and five million acres of rich alluvial deposit, which
cannot be surpassed in fertility. These are generally situated
along the water-courses and near the tides. These latter lands,
when dyked, yield enormous crops and require no dressing during
the life of at least one generation. The expense of building
dykes does not exceed that of clearing lightly timbered land, say
from $3 to $10 per acre, and the land once reclaimed requires no
more attention than saving and harvesting the crops. Farmers
who have taken pre-emption or homestead claims upon such land
and worked it for a year or two have been offered from three to

four thousand dollars for them. The bottom lands are easily cleared, the wood upon them being principally maple, crabapple, alder, ash and an occasional cedar, spruce or fir tree. The valley of the Skagit river is extensive enough to furnish farms for at least five thousand persons. The Lummi valley, near the Skagit, is twenty miles long and two miles wide and but thinly settled, so that it offers excellent inducements for those seeking homes. In fact, happy homes can be made on any of the principal rivers and valleys, throughout Washington, from its most southern to its most northern limits. Such land as belongs to the Northern Pacific Railroad Company, which is every odd section for twenty miles on each side of the surveyed line of the railroad, is open to settlers, and all unsurveyed land belonging to it, which may be occupied by persons, can be purchased as soon as it is appraised, the settler having the first privilege of buying. The land in Yakima, Colville and Walla Walla valleys in Eastern Washington, are excellent grain and grazing lands, and those desirous of engaging in stock-raising can find no better country in the world. Bunch grass, native to the country, abounds and retains a perennial nutrition. Water is plenty and thousands of animals brouse the year round and are always in the best condition. Whatever portion of the Territory an immigrant may scan, he will find there, with rare exceptions, desirable places on which to locate a home. Improved farms can be purchased, by such persons as do not wish to hew out a farm in the forest, and they have a variety of topography and climate to choose from, that must suit the most fastidious. They have the rolling plains and warm climate of Eastern Washington, with its numerous beautiful rivers and lakes, or the more humid and heavily timbered Western Washington, with its great bodies of water. The poor man, desirous of making a home for himself and family, and willing to work, can find no country which offers greater inducements than Washington Territory. He must not expect to find an earthly paradise, but he will find it superior to any of the States of the Atlantic coast. Ready facilities for the procuring of the public lands are offered, there being three land offices, at Olympia, Vancouver and Walla Walla, respectively.

SCHOOL AND SCHOOL LAWS.

The Territory is well supplied with schools, considering the sparseness of the population, and the number is constantly augmenting, as an increased interest is manifested in education from year to year, both by the people and the Legislature. There is a Territorial Superintendent of Common Schools, whose duty it is to look after the general welfare of schools, examine teachers, disseminate intelligence in reference to education throughout the Territory. For the support of schools the County Commissioners levy a tax of four mills on the dollar on all assessible property, and the principal of all moneys accruing from the sale of lands given, or which may be given for school purposes, by Congress, is made an irreducible fund, the interest of which shall be divided annually among the school districts in proportion to the number of school children they contain. Teachers are required to procure a certificate of qualification and good moral character before entering upon their duties. No books of a sectarian character allowed, nor any denominational doctrine taught in the schools. The following approximate totals will give an idea of the number of schools in the Territory and the salaries paid to teachers: Number of school houses, 172; school districts, 225; schools taught, 172; number of scholars attending, 4,792; persons of school age, 8,537; amount paid to teachers, $39,294 14. The following text books are in use in the schools: Sander's Union Speller and Reader, Robinson's Arithemetic and Algebra, Monteith's Geography, Kerl's Grammer, Spenser's writing and drawing books. There are several good private schools in the larger towns. The higher branches are taught at the Union Academy at Olympia, and the Territorial University at Seattle. This last is under the control of a Board of Regents, whose duty it is to apply the funds of accruing from the lands donated for its support, by act of Congress, which consist of 46,080 acres of selected lands, and look after its general welfare. Both male and female students are received.

PUBLIC BUILDINGS.

The Territory is yet to young to make any pretensions to architectual display, either in public or private buildings. Of the former, it may be said to have scarcely any. The Capitol building, situated at Olympia, is a square two-story, wooden building located in the suburbs. It has recently been repaired and greatly improved both inside and out, by an appropriation from the Federal Government of about $5,000.

The Territorial Penitentiary is located on McNeil's Island in Puget Sound, a few miles distant from Steilacoom. The Insane Asylum is also located at Steilacoom.

The Custom House is at Port Townsend. The Territorial University at Seattle is a wooden building, two stories high, rectangular in form, with columns in front. It was erected in 1863, at a cost of $60,000.

RAILROADS.

The first attempt at building a railroad in the Territory was made in 1871, and now four are in process of construction. One runs from Walla Walla to Wallula, a distance of thirty miles; another is the Pacific branch of the Northern Pacific Railroad, at present running from Kalama, on the Columbia River, to Tacoma, on Puget Sound. The third and fourth have their roads partially graded. The first of these, will run from Olympia to Tenino, a station on the N. P. R. R., and the second, from Seattle to Walla Walla. When these roads are finished, the Territory will have what it has long needed, a rapid means of transportation for its abundant products.

INDIANS.

The Indians of the Territory, like the race in every part of the country, are rapidly fading away before the advance of civilization. The Territory had a very large Indian population, a few years ago, but the number will not now reach fifteen thousand souls, and they are rapidly decimating through sickness and the vices learned from the white men.   The principal portion of the Indians are confined to the reservations, and many of them raise fruits, grains and stock, while others work round mills, logging camps and farms.   The outside laborers earn from one to two dollars a day, and during the "seal season" they earn as high as forty dollars a day hunting the fur seal.   There are fourteen reservations in the Territory, and they contain from five hundred to four thousand each, and all are under the charge of superintendents.   Each reservation has its church and school-house.   The natives are quiet and industrious, inclined to be religious, punctual at service and comparatively free from vice.   The Government furnishes teachers, overseers, surgeons, chaplains, and such other persons as may be required to look after their welfare.

NOTES TO IMMIGRANTS.

There is no portion of the country, perhaps, that offers all the advantages to an immigrant equal to this Territory.   The lands along the water courses are extremely fertile, and these are very numerous; its tide lands make the finest gardens in the world when dyked, and produce extensive crops.   Its timber lands are useful both for agriculture and commercial purposes, and its prairies afford good pasturage for all domestic animals.   These lands, of all grades, can be found in the Territory.   They can be purchased, pre-empted or taken up under the homestead act, so that he who desires to labor, and is willing to make a home for himself, can find the means in this genial country.   The person desiring to take up a farm along the courses of the rivers, can find plenty of room and land, from Lumni on the north to the lower portion of the Columbia.   Timber land can be found any where in Western Washington, except near the milling towns, and if it is adjacent to water it is valuable, as loggers get about five dollars a thousand for saw-logs, and they select such land as will afford them ready facilities of getting their timber to water.

C

They pay fifty cents per thousand feet for stumpage, so that a person having heavily timbered land can receive double compensation from it; first, from the lumber, then from the products raised. Some of this class of land is difficult and expensive to clear, but much of it is comparatively easy and inexpensive. The principal prairies are in Eastern Washington, and they are undoubtedly the best grazing lands in the world, being covered with the large and abundant bunch grass, which retains its nutrition the year round. These prairies are traversed by thousands of domestic animals, who roam at large, with little or no care from their owners. The immigrant desirous of following the business, will find here ample room. The smaller prairies afford excellent opportunities for engaging in the wool business. Wool brings a good price, mutton is always sought for in the market, and wild animals destructive to sheep are scarce. Were an immigrant to ask, where can I find a good farm, we would say: Almost any where in Washington Territory. Go where you may, you can find land in its primitive state or under cultivation. As to the healthfulness of the country, it is unequaled by any portion of the Union and the truth of this statement can be learned, at any time, by reference to the report of the Surgeon-General of the United States. The resources of the country are yet undeveloped. Commerce, with the exception of the lumber and coal trade, is dormant, and manufactories comparatively unknown. The Territory does the largest lumber trade in the world, and ships, laden with spars, masts and lumber can be seen daily on their way through the waters of the Sound. The minerals of the Territory, which are rich and varied, have not, with the exception of coal, been developed at all. House rent is comparatively small, churches are plentiful, and the facilities for education are excellent. Those desiring to furnish their children an ample education can do so, as all the larger towns are liberally supplied with private and public schools. The population of the Territory is composed largely of natives of the New England and Middle States, but like every other portion of the country, representatives of European nationalities are found here. A more orderly and law-abiding population cannot be found in America.

Private and benevolent societies are numerous and large in numbers. All the principal denominations have churches throughout the Territory, so that the immigrant can find here, as well as in his native land, the consolations of his faith. While thus showing the advantages of the country, we would not advise all who desire to better their conditions to flock here, unless they are willing to toil, and are possessed of courage and endurance to hew themselves a home out of the forests and labor for the advancement of the country. Those persons engaged in the lighter occupations, such as professional men, book-keepers and clerks, will not find much employment, until the commerce and population of the Territory increase. Farmers, mechanics, carpenters, masons and blacksmiths are most needed, as they are useful in every community. Gentlemen of leisure, and their kindred are not wanted. The country is yet too young to support drones of any kind. People wanted then, are the earnest, hard working kind, who have an object in life and wishing to make preparations for their families and old age. Those who come, need not expect to find all they desire immediately; they must be content, if they take farms, to live somewhat isolated for a short time, unless they have means to purchase land in more thickly settled districts. But this isolation must be for a short time only, as these fertile lands cannot remain long unsettled. The inhabitants of Europe and the Eastern States are seeking more elbow room, and to the "Great West" they must come. He is the best off, then, who comes first and has the privilege of making a selection of the lands, and he will find that Washington possesses all the elements of a great and prosperous State, and offers superior inducements to those seeking homes.

RATES OF WAGES.

Many persons, doubtless, would be glad to know what class of mechanics, laborers and domestic servants are needed in the country, and the wages paid. To the first query, we would say, that any person able and willing to work, can find employment. The persons most needed are farmers, who are willing to hew

themselves a home with their brawny arms, or have the means
of improving land. Manufacturers are wanted to utalize in the
oountry the productions .of the country, and thus enrich that
which should be enriched, and not allow all the profits and con-
trol of the commerce to fall into the hands of those who have no
interest in the advancement of the Territory. Mechanics are
wanted, blacksmiths and carpenters make from three to five dollars per day in gold. Boiler-makers and machinists receive from
five to seven dollars per day, but the demand for their services
is at present limited. Good waiters get a salary ranging from
thirty-five to forty dollars a month and board. Day laborers,
receive from forty to sixty dollars per month, and many are required to work around mills and logging-camps and to work on
wagon-roads. Good axemen, as loggers, get from sixty to one
hundred dollars per month and board. Teamsters about the
same, and mill-hands from thirty-five to fifty dollars per month
with board. Cooks receive from fifty to one hundred dollars a
month and board; clerks from sixty to one hundred dollars and
book-keepers average one hundred dollars a month, but few of
the latter class are needed at present. Sailors get thirty-five
dollars a month on coasting vessels and twenty on foreign.
School and music teachers are not in good demand and the wages
paid are small. Female servants for the house are much needed
and are paid better, proportionately, than any other class of employees. One hundred girls could find positions of this class,
within a week after their arrival in the Territory, at from twenty
to thirty-five dollars per month and board. Literary men and
loiterers are not wanted and had better keep away. The motto
that " fortune favors the brave," will be found a good one here,
for it is only the brave of heart, the ready, willing toiler that is
desired. He is needed to advance the country, to help place it
among the first of the States of the Union. It possesses dormant wealth and resources, all that is required is their develop-
ment. Kid-gloved men, persons of extremely fine sensibilities
are not the characters to develop these, but the hardy, laborious
and courageous man who fears not toil, and is willing to work
hard at present that he may enjoy his ease hereafter.

DESCRIPTION BY COUNTIES.

The Territory Described by Counties.

WHATCOM COUNTY.

The boundaries of this extreme north-western county are British Columbia on the north, the Cascade Mountains on the east, Snohomish County on the south and St. George's Channel and Canal de Haro on the west. It is the largest county west of the Cascade Mountains and contains half a million acres of agricultural land ot which not one-fifth is owned or occupied. There are three classes of land, viz.: tide marsh, (of which there is the largest body of any county in the Territory), river bottom and high, rolling land. The average soil is a rich brown loam, resting upon a heavy sub-soil of clay and will produce from 40 to 80 bushels of wheat, 100 bushels of oats or barley and from 200 to 500 bushels of potatoes per acre. Every kind of fruit and vegetable is grown here, usually found in a temperate climate, in great perfection. The timber of the county is pine, (on the mountains), fir, cedar, spruce, maple and alder. There are several first-class water powers here, fine sites for steam mills and a good opening for a grist mill, a saw mill and a woolen mill. The Bellingham Bay coal mine is located here. An inexhaustible supply of clay fit for earthenware, quarries of fine sandstone for building purposes and on account of its eligibility of position and timber, this must naturally become a point for shipbuilding at no distant day. There are fifteen schools and one saw mill, and mail communication once a week with the outside world. Bordering upon British Columbia, a ready market for surplus products is here found. Improved lands in this county are worth from $3 50 to $15 00 per acre. The principal towns are What-com, Schome and La Conner. The estimated population is 1,400; the taxable property, $469,277 and the area in square miles about 3,840.

SAN JUAN COUNTY.

The county of San Juan is an archipelago lying between Van-couver Island, B. C., on the west and Whatcom county on the east. It offers many excellent opportunities for immigrants and much of its best land lies unoccupied—land that is easily cleared and will produce heavy crops of either grain or vegetables. San Juan, the principal island, is already thickly settled, still there are some good claims to be had and several improved farms can be bought at a reasonable figure. There are two schools here and excellent instructors teach in each, during six months of the year. Divine service is held every Sunday. There are also two stores and a blacksmith shop and roads traverse the island from one end to the other. Lopez Island is smaller than San Juan, but has a larger amount of agricultural land, in proportion to its size, than the latter. Most of the land claimed on Lopez, is at, or near the water, leaving the interior, which is really the finest land, lying idle. Here can be found large and beautiful alder bottoms, marshes and fern lands, all of which are very easily brought under cultivation, and once cultivated, they produce equal to any land in the country. There is but one school upon this island. There is a store and a post-office, to which roads lead from all parts of the island. Good claims can also be found on seve-ral other islands, Orcas, Stewart, John's, Decatur, and others. Some of these are excellent for sheep-raising as well as farming. The population of the county is 533, the taxable property, $132,848, and the area in square miles about 280.

ISLAND COUNTY.

This county lies at the mouth of Admiralty Inlet, (an arm of Puget Sound) and consists of two islands, Camano and Whidby.

Whidby contains 115,000 acres of land and Camano nearly 30,-000. All of Camano, except 2,000 or 3,000 acres and two-thirds of Whidby, are heavily timbered with fir, cedar, hemlock, spruce and alder. The remainder consists of natural prairies and re-claimed swamp lands, above the average in fertility, producing largely of wheat, barley, oats, hay, fruit and garden vegetables, when properly cultivated. Much of the timber land is fit for grazing when cleared, producing good blue-grass, timothy and clover. About half the population are engaged in farming and the remainder in lumbering and commercial pursuits. There are Government lands in the county, but good farming lands may be bought at reasonable figures. There are six schools in the county and one church and mail facilities are good. There is one large saw mill at Utsalady and a flouring mill at Coveland. Coupeville and Oak Harbor are also towns of some importance. The taxable property of the county is $460,363; population, 580 and it has an area of 250 square miles.

SNOHOMISH COUNTY.

This county has for boundaries Whatcom County on the north, the waters of Puget Sound on the west, King County on the south and the Cascade Mountains on the east. It is heavily timbered with fir, cedar, alder, maple, etc., except on the tide flats and marshes bordering on the Sound and at the mouth of its two great rivers—the Snohomish and Stillaguamish, which with their tributaries run through this region, making it one of the most fertile counties in the Territory. 2,600 acres of land have already been cleared for cultivation and 3,000 more are partially cleared and in use for pasturage. The principal grain region is upon the tide flats, and it is estimated that during last season (1874) about 18,000 bushels of oats and barley and 2,000 bushels of wheat were raised on the Stillaguamish flats alone. Besides feeding to stock a large quantity of oats and barley in the straw on the Snohomish, there were 3,000 bushels threshed and about 1,000 bushels of wheat. The principal hay region is in the river bottoms, and over 2,000 tons were raised there last year. The vegetables of the county are remarkable for size and quality, and enormous crops are harvested. At Snohomish City and Lowell, the principal towns, are located enterprising and intelligent communities. The foundations are here being laid morally, intellectually and financially, for flourishing cities at no distant day. The population of this county is 825, with children enough for eight school districts. The taxable property is $239,629 and possesses area of about 2,000 square miles, three-quarters of which is unexplored.

CLALLAM COUNTY.

This county is bounded on the north by the Straits of San Juan de Fuca, east and south by Jefferson county and on the west by the Pacific Ocean. The soil is varied, but in general it is good and well adapted to ordinary farming. All kinds of crops found in a temperate climate are grown here advantageously. Wheat, barley and potatoes yield enormously, and it is not uncommon to harvest a good volunteer crop of grain from fields which the year before produced 80 and 90 bushels to the acre. The timber of the county is large and fine, principally fir, cedar and hemlock. Good farming land awaits the settler a few miles back from the bays and rivers, nearly all the front claims having been taken up. There are three regularly organized school districts and good school buildings. There are no churches and but one religious body—the Methodists—who have services once a month and religious services are held by a visiting clergyman of the Episcopal church, as often as every other Sunday, at the Courthouse at New Dunginess. Mails are received weekly. Logging and farming are the principal industries, and the class of immigrants most likely to succeed here, are those acquainted with one of these, and men of muscle and energy generally. The roads are good, the general face of the country being level, making the shipping and hauling of produce easy. The Government lands in the county are but $1 25 per acre. Improved lands are worth from $3 00 to $10 00 per acre. The population of the county is 351, taxable property, $126,905 and an area of 2,050 square miles, half unexplored.

––––

JEFFERSON COUNTY.

The boundaries of Jefferson are the Straits of Juan de Fuca and Clallam county on the north, the waters of Puget Sound on the east, Mason and Chehalis counties on the south and the Pacific Ocean on the west. The general character of the country is rough and but a small per cent. of the land is suitable for agriculture, though quite a number of farms have been opened up in the several valleys and there is still much good land unoccupied. There are but few good farms for sale in the county, but good land, still unimproved, can be bought at from $3 00 to $12 00 per acre, and there is Government land subject to pre-emption and homestead entries. Lumbering is the chief industry, though there is a good market at the county seat, Port Townsend and the milling points, for all produce raised, at good prices. Lumbermen and mill-hands are in demand, and domestic servants are much needed here. Chinamen are employed, where in nearly every case, white help would be preferred. The public schools in this county rank among the first in the Territory. There are four churches at Port Townsend and divine services are held at all the milling towns and farming settlements. There are four post offices in the county, with semi-weekly mail to each, and telegraphic communication is established with the outside world. Port Townsend is the port of entry for Washington Territory and is on the line of the principal steamboat routes. The sub-District Court also convenes here. Two lumber mills are located in this county, one at Port Discovery and one at Port Ludlow. The population of the county is 1,208, the taxable property, $495,264 and the area about 2,000 square miles, probably three-fourths of which is practically unexplored.

KITSAP COUNTY.

This county is a peninsula bounded on the north, west and east by Puget Sound and south by Pierce and Mason counties. It is a heavily wooded region and is noted as being the county in which are located a large number of the great lumber mills of Puget Sound; in fact it is the milling county of the Territory. Six mills of great capacity are located here and constantly employ a large number of men. At Port Gamble are two lumber mills, one of which has a capacity of 240,000 feet per day and is probably the largest lumber mill in the world, and a grist mill, and at Port Madison, Port Blakely and Seabeck are lumber mills. At each of these points are flourishing towns with excellent church and school facilities, temperance organizations, etc. The population of this county is estimated at 1,300, taxable property, $789,029, area in square miles about 540.

KING COUNTY.

The boundaries of this county are as follows: North by Snohomish, east by the Cascade Mountains, south by Pierce county and west by the waters of Puget Sound. It is one of the most important counties in the Territory on account of its mineral, agricultural and commercial resources. Its mineral wealth cannot as yet be estimated, although it is known to be great, as much of the county lying among the foot-hills of the Cascade Mountains has never been explored, but its vast coal-fields are already yielding a large revenue to the companies engaged in working them. This is owing to the facilities for easy transportation that is afforded by the lakes and rivers which abound in the county, forming a complete net-work of navigable waters. The outlet of these waters is through the Duwamish river into Elliott Bay, on which is situated Seattle, the largest and most thriving town on Puget Sound. It is very eligibly located for commerce, has a tolerably good harbor and is well supplied with wharves and warehouses. Manufactories of various kinds are carried on and merchants, doctors and lawyers, thrive here; hotels and restaurants are well patronized and the various churches and schools are in a flourishing condition. Lake Washington, on which is situated one of the principal coal mines in the Territory, is a large and beautiful lake, lying a few miles from Seattle in an easterly direction and is connected with Lake Union (lying about a mile from Seattle) by a short portage. Over this portage and to the wharf where it is loaded into ships, the coal is carried over a railroad. A railroad to the Talbot mine on Black River is also in process of construction. Around Lake Washington and indeed all the lakes of the county, there is more or less rich agricultural land, and the river bottoms cannot be exceeded in fertility. The uplands of King county are covered with a heavy growth of fir and cedar, but all through the county, interspersed here and there, are swales, swampy lands and prairies, equal in richness, to the river bottoms, thus giving the enterprising immigrant a chance for locating in any part of the county and the industrious mechanic and artisan of the Eastern States and the hardy pioneer of the West, may alike find homes in our genial and salubrious climate. The population is 3,500, taxable property, $1,778,172. Area in square miles about 1,900.

MASON COUNTY.

The county is bounded by Jefferson and Kitsap counties on the north, on the east by Kitsap, Pierce and Thurston, on the south by Thurston and Chehalis. About three-fourths of this county is more or less hilly, and some of it mountainous. A small portion of the upland is fertile, such as is covered with a growth of hemlock, cedar, alder and maple. There are several valleys of good land yet unoccupied. The largest tracts of which are on the Skokomish and Satsop rivers and Goldsborough creek. There are several prairies, which would make excellent stock ranges, and enough good land in the county for many fair sized neighborhoods, which can be had of the Government or bought of the N. P. R. R. Co., at about Government prices.

Yellow fir, hemlock and cedar is the timber of the uplands; spruce, alder, maple, ash and cottonwood of the bottoms. Stock raising is carried on here successfully. Hay is the principal crop raised, though grains, vegetables and fruit do well here. The class of immigrants needed is families—those with energy, who are not afraid of hard work. Persons coming here to make homes must not expect to get them close to the bay, for nearly all the good land bordering the shore is already taken; they will have to go back from four to ten miles for farm lands. Mail communications once a week and the roads very good, though most of the travel and all the freighting is done by water. There are but few schools and no churches in the county. The principal towns are Arcadia, Oakland and Union City. The taxable property of the county is $178,510, the population 400, and the area 900 square miles, about half of which is unexplored.

CHEHALIS COUNTY.

The boundaries of this county are Jefferson and Mason counties on the north, Mason, Thurston and Lewis on the east, Lewis and Pacific on the south and the Pacific Ocean on the west. The land may be divided into three classes: River bottom, prairie and upland. The river bottoms amount to, perhaps, one-third of the county and are very fertile, having been known to produce 60 bushels of wheat to the acre, with an average of 40, 20 to 40 bushels of barley, 50 to 80 of oats and all vegetables for culinary purposes yield large and fine crops. The soil of this land is clay loam with more or less sand. The prairie lands lie at various heights above the bottoms and produce good crops of grain, vegetables and grass, but are used principally far pasturage. The upland is for the most part rough, though it has some good soil. The timber of the bottoms is vine-maple, cottonwood, salmon-brush, alder and maple, with a few spruces and firs. Much of this class of land may be cleared at a cost of $15 per acre. The uplands are mainly covered with fir, spruce, cedar and hemlock, which are noted for their fine quality. Land fit for cultivation may be estimated at about two-thirds the whole county, and the amount in private hands at about one-fourth. The price per acre, for unimproved lands is from $1 25 to $5; improved, from $10 to $20 per acre. The principal industries of the county are dairying, raising beef, grain and other farm products. The butter of this region, known in the market as the Chehalis butter is dense and yellow at all seasons of the year and commands a higher price than any other grade. Persons engaged in this business make from three or four hundred pounds, to a ton, during the season, which finds a ready market at from 25 to 50 cents per pound. A grist mill is greatly needed here and mill sites are plenty. Energetic and industrious people are wanted as settlers in Chehalis county and farmers more than any other class. The roads are tolerably good, considering the land upon which they are made. Rich land always makes some mud in wet weather when much traveled over. The county is well supplied with game, such as elk, deer, ducks and geese. Schools and churches are abundant and the inhabitants are of good moral character. There is a regular mail to all the post-offices in the county. Elma and Montesano are two of the most important and thriving towns. The taxable property amounts to $301,799, estimated population 750, and an area of about 2,800 square miles, probably one-half of which is not thoroughly explored.

PIERCE COUNTY.

The boundaries of this county are as follows: North by King and Kitsap counties, west by Thurston and Puget Sound, south by Thurston and Lewis and east by the Cascade Mountains. Stock and hop raising are among the principal industries of this section. Four hundred acres in the rich Puyallup valley were this year devoted to the cultivation of hops, with a probable yield of 100,000 pounds. This region is also attracting considerable attention on account of the deposits of bituminous and (it is claimed) anthracite coal of fine quality found here, which, when developed, must add greatly to the wealth of the county. The-terminus of the Northern Pacific Railroad on Puget Sound, is located at Tacoma and the company have spent considerable money to improve this point. At Tacoma (the old town) is also located a first-class lumber mill with a capacity of 60,000 feet per day. At Steilacoom is situated the Territorial Insane Asylum and upon McNeil's Island near Steilacoom stretches a graveled prairie, scattered over which are numerous lakes and groves rendering it a beautiful spot and a famous place of resort for its magnificent drives as well as its lovely scenery. Much good agricultural land is still to be found vacant in the county and is open to the settler. The population of the county is 1,800; taxable property, $1,123,062 72 and an area of about 1,800 square miles, one-half of which is practically unexplored.

THURSTON COUNTY.

Thurston county is bounded on the north by Mason and Pierce counties and the waters of Puget Sound. Its general character is timbered with a large amount of bottom land, much of which has been overflowed for years by beavers and will require draining; it will then make the best land for grass and after a few years for grain and vegetables. The principal productions are hay and stock. The dairy also pays well. Wheat, oats, rye and barley are raised in some localities and potatoes, parsnips, beets, carrots, turnips, cabbage, etc., yield very large crops. It has always been supposed that corn could not be grown with profit in this county, but recent experiments have demonstrated, that on sandy land with good cultivation, it will pay as well, or better, than any other crop. The principal fruits of the county are apples, pears, plums, cherries, currants, raspberries, strawberries, etc. The red, black and blue huckleberry, blackberry, cranberry, sallal, salmonberry, and Oregon grape, grow wild in great abundance. It is considered that nearly all the county is fit for agricultural and grazing purposes, but a large amount of it will not pay for clearing for farms, until such a time as there will be a demand for lumber, then the timber will pay for the clearing. It will then be valuable land, surpassing in many instances, the highly cultivated land of New York and Ohio. The timber is fir, cedar, maple, alder and a little oak and white ash. There is an immense water power at Tumwater, where are located two flouring mills, one saw-mill, one water-pipe manufactory, one tannery, a sash and door factory, etc., and there is power for an immense amount of additional machinery. At Olympia is located the capital of the Territory and the various U. S. offices. School and church facilities are numerous and the roads excellent. Steam communication with the upper Sound is had nearly every day and there is a daily mail with the East. The population of the county is 2,359; taxable property, $1,358,537 and an area of about 720 square miles, one-eighth of which is unexplored.

LEWIS COUNTY.

This county's boundaries are Thurston and Chehalis counties on the north, the Cascade Mountains on the east, Skamania, Cowlitz and Wahkiakum counties on the south, Wakiakum and Pacific on the west. Its general character is ridge and bottom lands. The soil is a clay and clay loam. The ridges are heavily timbered with cedar, fir, some alder, maple and other small timber; the bottoms are covered with brush, dogwood, vine maple and wild cherry. Wheat, oats and barley are grown here with a large yield when properly cultivated, and hay from two to five tons per acre and vegetables and fruit large and good. The N. P. R. R. runs through this section of the country, which with the Cowlitz river and tolerably good wagon roads, afford ample means of transportation. Churches, schools and post-offices are within reach of all the settlers; mails by railroad. Large bodies of tillable land await the settler; extensive coal fields abound; available and well situated water-powers are numerous and yet unimproved, and plenty of good timber. Chehalis is the county seat. Improved lands are worth from $2 50 to $40 per acre, unim-

D

proved from $2 50 to $5, according to location. The population of the county is 1,500; taxable property, $1,155,650; area in square miles about 1,800, probably one-half of which is unexplored.

PACIFIC COUNTY.

This county's boundaries are as follows: North by Chehalis county, east by Lewis and Wahkiakum, south by the Columbia river and west by the Pacific Ocean. It is the south-western county of the Territory, and contains a large amount of good land on the rivers and bays, a portion only of which is settled up, leaving a large quantity that is yet vacant. In the country along the Columbia there are several fisheries and room for hundreds more, a business which is rapidly increasing in importance and will certainly yield immense fortunes. At Centerville, on the Columbia, is a saw-mill which furnishes a large amount of lumber for the San Francisco markets. At Oysterville, the county seat, located on Shoalwater Bay, 20 miles north of the Columbia and on the coast, are the great oyster-beds which supply the Portland and San Francisco markets with this luxury. The oyster trade is engaged in by many of the citizens who are doing well and some are making fortunes in the business. Oysterville is a beautiful little town, with its church and school-house showing the evidences of civilization. The entrance to Shoalwater Bay is good, so that ships and steamers get in and out readily. There are quite a number of small rivers emptying into this bay, on which can be found good water-powers for mills of any kind. But little snow ever falls in this locality, the winters are mild and the climate not to be excelled for health. The opening for those who want to find homes is good, as there is a large amount of excellent agricultural land vacant in the county, and Government land at $1 25 per acre. The taxable property of the county is $322,945; population, 750 and an area in square miles of about 550, one-quarter of which is still unexplored.

WAHKIAKUM COUNTY.

This county is bounded as follows: North by Lewis, west by Pacific county, east by Lewis and Cowlitz and south by the Columbia. A heavily timbered country, mostly hills and mountains. The amount fit for agriculture is very small. About all the land fit for cultivation is already settled. Amount in private hands, 6,048 acres. Scarcely any improved land is sold; unimproved lands sell at from $2 50 to $5 00 per acre. The general product of the land is hay, potatoes, rutabagas, and garden vegetables. Little grain is raised; potatoes yield from 200 to 300 bushels per acre; hay, 2 to 4 tons. Timber—yellow fir, hemlock, spruce, curly maple, cottonwood, cedar and alder; the tide lands are timbered with spruce; the uplands with all the kinds before mentioned. Three logging-camps are engaged in getting out yellow fir and spruce logs, which are towed to Portland and nearer points. The catching, salting and canning of salmon is the peculiar industry of the county. There are six canneries now running, which employ from 100 to 200 men each. Fully 1,000 men and boys could get profitable employment about the canneries during the months of May, June and July, if it were not for the Chinamen. About three-fourths of the employees are Chinamen, who get (at Cathlamet) $1 a day, without board. White men get $40 to $50 per month and board; wages paid to hay harvest hands, $2 a day and board. The poorer class of immigrants could get little homes here, if they would turn fishermen part of the year, and improve their lands at other times. Schools, four; they are all small; teachers' wages, $20 to $30 a month and board. Only one church—Catholic—services seldom. Tri-weekly mail via the Columbia post-offices, Eagle Cliff, Waterford, Cathlamet and Skomokawa. Three or four short wagon roads leading from the claims in the Elohomon and Skomokawa valleys to the Columbia. A cool, healthy climate, good grass and water, just the thing for dairying. The population of this county is 600; taxable property, $172,-761, and the area about 360 square miles, one-fourth unexplored.

COWLITZ COUNTY.

This county's boundaries are as follows: North by Lewis and Wahkiakum counties, east by Skamania, south by Clark and the Columbia river and west by Wahkiakum. It is one of the tier of counties lying on the Columbia river, of which Kalama (the southern terminus of the Northern Pacific Railroad in Washington Territory) is the county seat. It is well located, having the benefit of the Columbia, Cowlitz and Lewis rivers and the Northern Pacific Railroad, making it convenient for farmers and business men, as they can get in and out at all times with their produce and merchandise. There is a great amount of good land in the county, much of which is yet vacant. The farmers are doing well in producing grain, vegetables and hay, and in raising stock. Cattle, sheep, hogs and horses thrive here and increase rapidly. This part of the country abounds in good timber, and among its exports beside wheat, oats, hay, potatoes, beef, mutton and pork, are lumber and maple knots. It has a long water-front on the Columbia river, and this will greatly enrich the county, as salmon are very abundant and easily secured. The class of immigrants most likely to succeed here would be industrious and hard-working farmers. Besides Kalama, Monticello and Freeport are towns of some importance. The population of the county is 2,000, taxable property, $644,259; area 1,100 square miles, about one-fourth of which is unexplored.

CLARKE COUNTY.

This county is bounded on the north by Cowlitz, east by Skamania and south and west by the Columbia river. The general character of the county is timbered, interspersed with openings and small prairies. Nearly all the land is fit for cultivation and the price of that already improved ranges from $10 to $20 per acre. The timber is fir, cedar, maple, hemlock, oak and ash. The county is fast filling up with an honest, hearty and industrious set of people. It has already a population of 900 voters and room for many more, though no one need to go there who is afraid of hard work. Wheat, oats, barley, rye, in fact all kinds of cereals, natural to a temperate climate, yield largely. School and church facilities are excellent and the wagon roads are said to be the best of any in the country west of the Cascade Mountains. There are several saw and grist mills here and room for more. Vancouver is the county seat and is a town of about 1,000 inhabitants. The whole population of the county is 3,584, taxable property amounts to $679,008 and an area of 725 square miles.

SKAMANIA COUNTY.

This county is bounded on the north by Lewis and Yakima counties, east by Yakima and Klickitat, south by Klickitat and west by Clarke, Cowlitz and Lewis. A greater part of it lies in the Cascade Mountains and on the Columbia river and is therefore rough, with but very little good farming land except on the river banks, which is mostly taken up. All kinds of grain can be raised, but grass and pasturage for cattle are the principal products and the county is well timbered, principally with fir. Six miles of railroad connect the upper and lower Cascades, over which all the freight which goes to Eastern Oregon, or up and down the Columbia river, must pass. Handling freight, cutting and hauling wood, keeping the railroad in repair, making butter and stock-raising are the principal industries. There are four school districts in the county and about eighty scholars. No churches or ministers. There is a daily mail carried by steamer and a wagon road from the Cascades to Clarke county and thence to the outside world. From the upper Cascades to the Dalles there is no road; travel is by trail and with boats. Eight or ten families have recently moved into the lower end of the county and there is still land enough for a good sized settlement. The population of the county is 166, taxable property, $124,911, and area about 2,300 square miles, three-fourths of which is unexplored.

KLICKITAT COUNTY.

The boundaries of this county are as follows: North by Yakima and Skamania, west by Skamania and south and east by the Columbia river. This county is in a good financial condition, being nearly out of debt and having a large school fund in proportion to the number of persons of school age. The soil is generally good, crop prospects good and a larger amount of acreage planted than ever before. The Klickitat valley is 20 by 30 miles in extent and is covered with a luxuriant growth of grass upon which stock keep fat eight or ten months of the year. Only a small portion of it is as yet settled and hundreds of claims await occupants. The Simcoe Mountains are covered with an inexhaustible supply of timber, principally pine, oak and fir. There are seven settlements in this valley alone, each having a school from six to eight months of the year. There are also two or three dry goods stores and several saw mills and blacksmith shops. Groceries and supplies can be had in the county at a small advance on Portland prices. The taxable property is $275,404, population 900, and area about 2,088 square miles, probably one-half of which is unexplored.

WALLA-WALLA COUNTY.

Walla-walla is bounded on the north by Whitman county, east by Columbia County, south by Oregon and west by the Columbia and Snake rivers. The climate is mild and healthy, the water excellent and abundant and the soil adapted to the production of grains, vegetables and fruits, such as are common to a temperate zone. This county is claimed to have produced more wheat in proportion, than any other in the United States; the whole crop of 1875 averaged 35 bushels to the acre. Several localities yielded as high as 57 bushels to the acre, one ten-acre field 85 to the acre, and one field of 150 acres produced 5,250— an average of 35 bushels, and this was a volunteer crop. Bunch grass covers the land not fit for grain, being very nutritious and plentiful during the entire year. Cattle for beef receive no other feed. The county is well adapted for wool-growing and both cattle and sheep are healthy and increase rapidly. There are a few weeks of hot and dusty weather in July, with the thermometer from 90 deg. to 105 deg., from one to three weeks of windy weather during the year, and a little freezing weather in Winter, but not more than one year in eight or ten, is it necessary to feed and shelter stock. Churches and schools are numerous, and the tone of society is moral. Walla-walla, the county seat, is the largest town in the Territory and a place of much importance. The taxable property of the county amounts to $1,992,065; number of square miles about 1,600, and the population in the vicinity of 5,000.

WHITMAN COUNTY.

The boundaries of this county are Idaho Territory on the east, Walla-walla county on the south, Columbia river on the west, and Stevens county on the north. It is principally rolling prairies with some hills and valleys. The valleys are not large but numerous, and the soil first-class. At least two-thirds of the entire area of the county is susceptible of cultivation and no county in the world is better watered. Not one-tenth of the arable land is yet taken or occupied. Improved lands may be bought at from $3 to $10 per acre, according to locality and amount of improvements. Great numbers of horses, cattle and sheep are raised here. Oats, wheat and barley, and in some localities corn, make a good crop and potatoes, turnips, carrots and other vegetables yield enormously. Flax, also is being sown to some extent. The timber of the county is confined principally to the streams and mountains and consists of cedar, larch, sugar pine, white pine, yew and some maple. The county has regularly organized school districts and school-houses are built as settlements require. At Colfax, the county seat, a flourishing school is established where all the higher English branches are taught, beside ancient and modern languages.   Mail facilities are good, roads superior and the healthfulness of the county is remarkable.   Two flour-mills and a saw-mill are doing a flourishing business here.   The taxable property of the county is $376,-887; the population is about 1,234 and the area, 4,300 square miles.

YAKIMA COUNTY.

Yakima county is bounded on the north by Stevens county, east by the Columbia river, south by Klickitat county and west by the Cascade Mountains. The general course of the Yakima river is from north-west. to south-east. At the mouth of the river there are some fine farms well adapted to grass or small grain. From this point to Cock's Ferry the country is very broken; back from the river a short distance the hills are covered with fine grass, but water is very scarce. A short distance from Cock's Ferry, and lying on the west side of the river, is the south-eastern boundary of the Simcoe Reservation, containing an area of twenty-five square miles of the best land on the river. The bluffs on the east side approach very near, and in many places quite to the river. The Tiatan river forms the northern boundary of the Reservation; it runs from west to east and empties into the Yakima river, at Yakima City. There is quite a large settlement on the river and many good farms. From Yakima City to the Natches river, the country is generally of second quality sage land, with a few pretty good farms on the river. Crossing the Natches you enter Selah valley, which is one of the most fertile in the county, though not large, containing probably, two or three sections of land. The Wenas creek runs from the north and empties into it, about three miles above the mouth of the Natches and on this stream there is quite an extensive valley of good land and many good farms. Leaving the Wenas, for twenty or thirty miles the land is very rolling and poor, until you reach the Kittitas valley, which is the largest body of good land except the Reservation, and this, like the Wenas valley, is settled by an agricultural population, and but for the heavy falls of snow it would be a very desirable country, being surrounded by low hills, covered with very fine pine timber. From this valley, the mountains set in and there is but little farming land above. For a reasonable amount of stock, Yakima county is a fine stock country in its present state, and by a provision for the winter, its capacity could be much extended. The population of this county is 1,200; taxable property, $413,167; area in square miles, 9,225.

STEVENS COUNTY.

The boundaries of this county are British Columbia on the north, the Bitter Root Mountains on the east, separating it from Idaho Territory, Whitman and Yakima counties on the south and the Cascade Mountains on the west. This county has some fertile and some very poor land. The Spokane plains are an extensive valley, a portion of which is rich land and covered with a heavy growth of very nutritious grass. The west side of the valley is bounded by very high and often steep bluffs, running to the Spokane river, and from this point to the head of Colville valley, the country is very poor, except that it has a dense growth of fine pine timber. Colville valley is entered at the head of a stream called Mill creek, which flows westward to old Fort Colville. This valley is capable of supporting several thousand persons, though some seasons it is rather frosty. It was originally settled by the Hudson Bay Company's servants, but they have gradually given place to Americans who have made extensive farms, and large crops of wheat, oats and barley are raised. The land on the south side of the Spokane river is of a very dark, rich loam and would support a large population, but occasionally crickets are troublesome here. Snow falls here to a greater depth than on the Colville side of the river. This part of Washington Territory is the most extensive grass-growing region and cannot for many years be overstocked. When the timber is left on the Spokane river, no more grass is found for several hundred miles, except limited quantities on the small streams. The area of this county, the largest in the Territory, is about 36,000 square miles, larger than Maine, and about as large as Kentucky. Three-fourths of this is unexplored. The population is 1,200, and taxable property, $253,526 50.

COLUMBIA COUNTY.

This county has just been set apart from Walla Walla by the Legislature of this year (1875). It is bounded on the north by Whitman county, east by Idaho Territory, south by Oregon and west by Walla Walla county. Dayton is the principal town and county seat and is a flourishing settlement. Here also is located the only woolen mill in the Territory, which manufactures 200,-000 pounds of wool per year, to the value of between $50,000 and $60,000. The climate is healthy and a large proportion of the soil is suitable for the production of all the grains, vegetables and fruits usually found in a temperate zone. Bunch grass is found upon the land not suitable for cultivation, and all kinds of stock thrive upon it, during the entire year. Not more than one winter in ten is it found necessary to feed or shelter stock. Church and school facilities are excellent. The population of the county is estimated at 3,000, and the taxable property at $800,000. The area in square miles is about 2,000.

Concluding Remarks.

THE PRESS OF THE TERRITORY.

There are fourteen newspapers published in the Territory, a fact which will give to the reader some idea of the intelligence and enterprise of the people. At Olympia, the capital, there are four weeklies and one daily issued, viz.: The Washington Standard, John Miller Murphy, editor and proprietor; weekly and Democratic in politics. The Olympia Transcript, E. T. Gunn, editor and proprietor; weekly and Independent in politics. The Puget Sound Courier, C. B. Bagley & Co., publishers; weekly and Republican in politics. The Morning Echo and Weekly Echo, Francis H. Cook, editor and proprietor; temperance in politics.

At Seattle, there are issued three weeklies and two dailies, viz.: Puget Sound Dispatch, daily and weekly, Beriah Brown & Co., publishers; Independent Republican in politics. The Pacific Tribune, daily and weekly, Thomas Prosch, editor and proprietor; Republican in politics.

At Steilacoom one weekly paper is published: The Puget Sound Express, Julius Dickens, editor and proprietor; Republican in politics.

At Port Townsend one newspaper, the Port Townsend Argus, C. W. Philbrick, editor and publisher, weekly and Republican in politics, is published.

At Whatcom one newspaper, the Bellingham Bay Mail, James Power, editor and publisher, weekly and Republican in politics, is published.

At Vancouver is issued the Vancouver Independent, W. Byron Daniels, editor; weekly and Independent in politics.

At Walla Walla, there are three papers published, viz.: The Spirit of the West, B. M. Washburne, editor; semi-weekly and Independent in politics. The Walla Walla Union, R. M. Smith & Co., publishers; weekly and Republican in politics. The Walla Walla Statesman, W. H. Newell, editor and proprietor; weekly and Independent in politics.

It will be observed that politics of every shade is here represented, and thus every man may rejoice in and support an organ advocating his own political faith.

———

BEST ROUTES TO WASHINGTON TERRITORY.

To reach Western Washington, the best, cheapest and most direct route for the immigrant, is by the Central and Union Pacific Railroads to San Francisco, and thence by sailing vessel or steamer to Puget Sound ports. Goodall, Nelson & Perkins and the Pacific Mail Steamship Co. are now running lines of steamers to the Sound at reduced rates, the numerous lumber ships of the Sound are constantly plying between its ports and San Francisco, and all of them carry passengers and freight, giving good accomodations.

To those who desire to reach Eastern Washington from parts as far east as Omaha, we would say that if they have teams of horses and wagons, and families, the best way is to come across the plains, in their own conveyances, provided they start early. There is plenty of grass and water, and no long dry drives now, as there used to be before the railroad was built. But for those starting late, or those having but small families, perhaps it would be as well to come by rail. Those not wishing to pay for first-class accommodation on the cars had better purchase through tickets at Omaha for San Francisco, either second or third class, and, when they reach Salt Lake, they can sell them at a premium, and purchase suitable conveyance, or else come on the stage, or on a passenger wagon. But, in no instance, would we advise persons bringing their own teams, to ship them by rail for any distance, except perhaps they should start very late in the season.

Those desiring to come from California will of course take the steamer at San Francisco, and have a safe and easy passage to Portland, when they must not pay too much attention to those who would attempt to lure them up the Willamette valley, which district annually sends us hundreds of immigrants. From Portland they can come up to Wallula, by steamboat at half fare, and from the latter point they can come on up to Walla Walla by stage or wagon now, or if they wait a short time they can come on the cars. When once here, we can assure the immigrant that he will be well treated, and will be furnished with all needful information concerning the country, in order to enable him to select his future abode.

FINIS.

ERRATUM.—On page 14, 8th line, for 800,000 read 80,000.

Index.